Pebble®
Plus

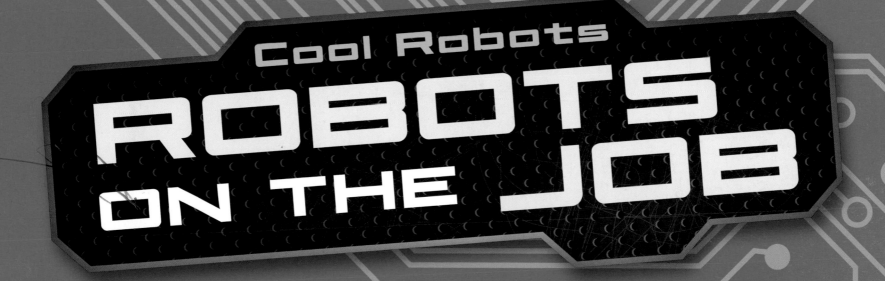

Cool Robots

ROBOTS ON THE JOB

by Kathryn Clay

Consulting Editor: Gail Saunders-Smith, PhD

Consultant: Seth Hutchinson, PhD
Department of Electrical and Computer Engineering
University of Illinois

CAPSTONE PRESS
a capstone imprint

Pebble Plus is published by Capstone Press,
1710 Roe Crest Drive, North Mankato, Minnesota 56003
www.capstonepub.com

Library of Congress Cataloging-in-Publication Data
Clay, Kathryn, author.
  Robots on the job / Kathryn Clay.
    pages cm.—(Pebble plus) (Cool robots)
  Summary: "Simple text and full-color photographs describe eight different industrial or military robots and the work these robots do."—Provided by publisher.
  Includes bibliographical references and index.
  ISBN 978-1-4914-0586-4 (hb)—ISBN 978-1-4914-0650-2 (pb)—ISBN 978-1-4914-0620-5 (eb)
  1. Robots—Juvenile literature. 2. Robotics—Juvenile literature. I. Title.
  TJ211.2.C557 2015
  629.8'92—dc23   2014002308

Editorial Credits
Erika L. Shores, editor; Terri Poburka, designer; Katy LaVigne, production specialist

Photo Credits
Alamy: Leslie Garland Picture Library, 11; Bloomberg via Getty Images: Kiyoshi Ota, 13; DoD photo by Spc. Michael J. MacLeod, U.S. Army, 19; Glow Images: Imagebroker/Jim West, cover; Newscom: EPA/Toshiki Sawaguchi, 7, Polaris/Nancy Ellison, 15, Reuters/John Gress, 17; Petman Robot image courtesy of Boston Dynamics, 9; Shutterstock: Dikiiy, 5; U.S. Navy photo by John F. Williams, 21

Design Elements
Shutterstock: Irena Peziene, Kate Pru

Note to Parents and Teachers

The Cool Robots set supports national science standards related to science, technology, engineering, and mathematics. This book describes and illustrates industrial and military robots. The images support early readers in understanding the text. The repetition of words and phrases helps early readers learn new words. This book also introduces early readers to subject-specific vocabulary words, which are defined in the Glossary section. Early readers may need assistance to read some words and to use the Table of Contents, Glossary, Read More, Internet Sites, and Index sections of the book.

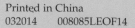
Printed in China
032014   008085LEOF14

Table of Contents

Robots at Work

Did you know robots work
in factories? Other robots
work in hospitals
or in the deep ocean.

Earthquakes can trap people under rubble. Robots such as Enryu could be sent to the rescue. Robotic arms can lift rubble out of the way.

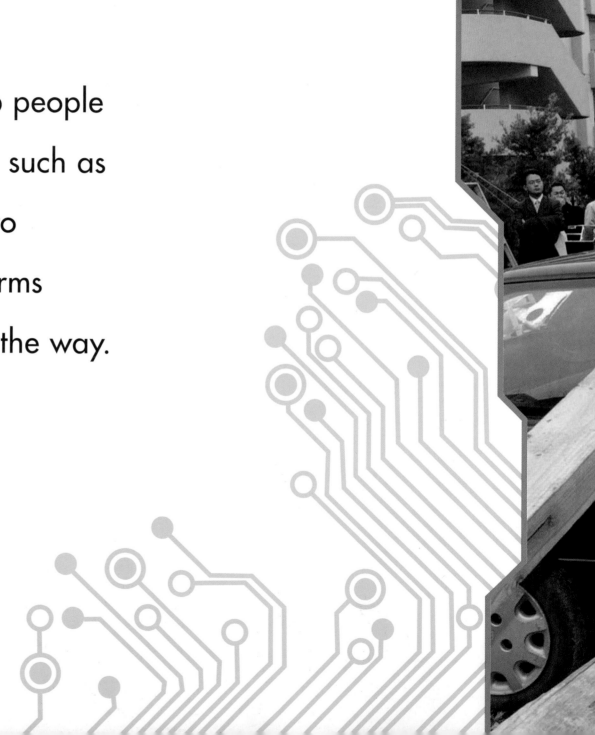

PETMAN looks like a human.

It walks, climbs stairs,

and does pushups.

The robot is used to test

clothing worn by soldiers.

Factory Robots

Robotic arms help build cars.

Large arms lift heavy objects.

Smaller arms pinch tweezers

or twist bolts.

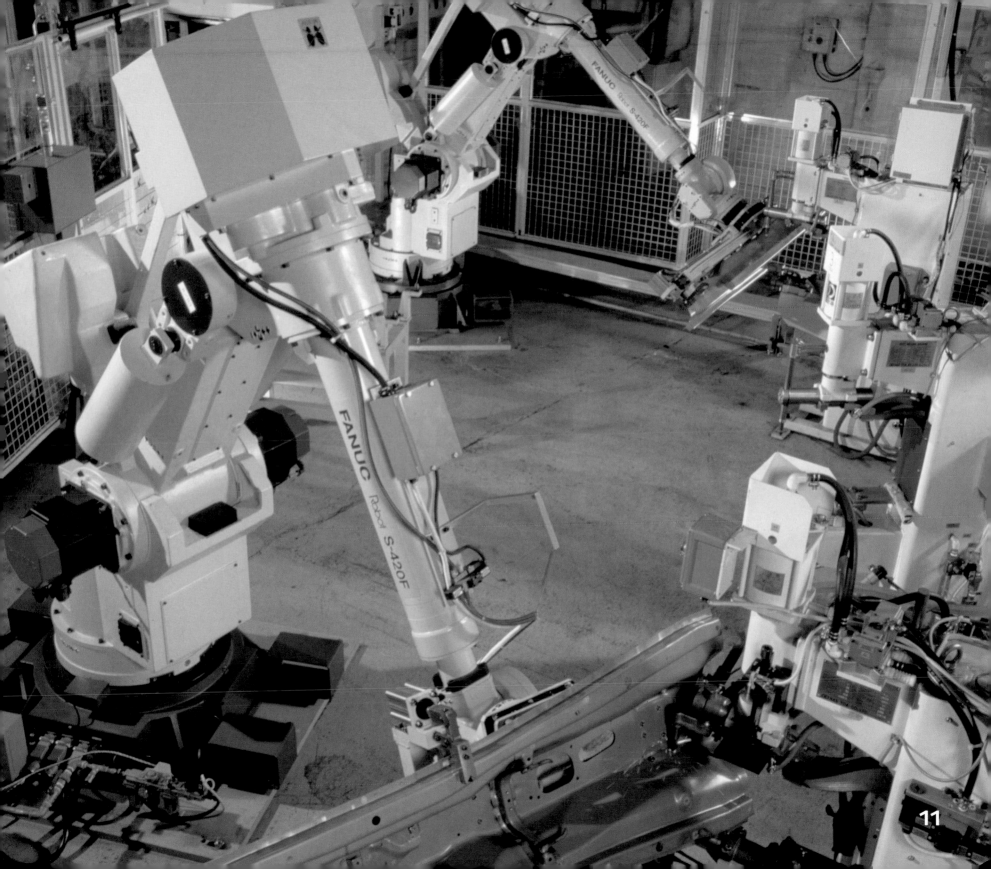

11

SushiBot grabs piles of rice.

It loads on vegetables and fish.

This speedy Japanese robot makes

300 sushi rolls each hour.

Medical Robots

Doctors use remote controls to guide the da Vinci Surgical System. Robotic arms make tiny cuts to reach a person's heart.

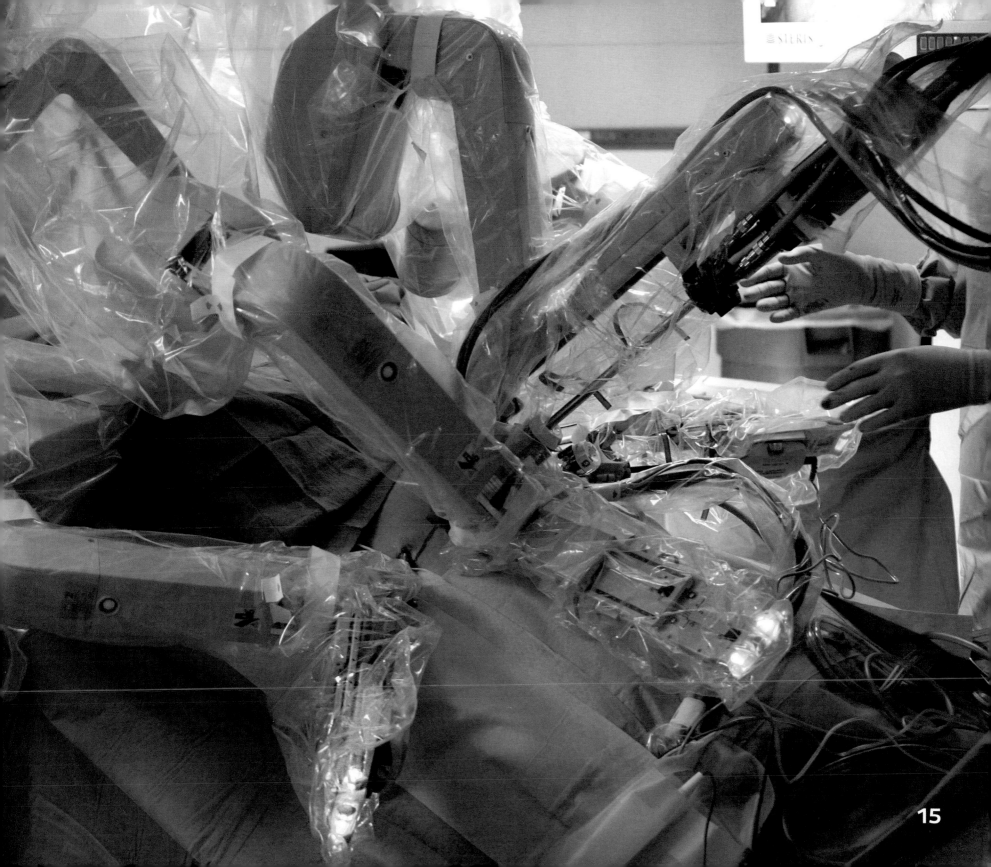

Scientists built a bionic leg.
Sensors in the robotic leg
get signals from the knee muscles.
The signals tell the bionic leg
how to move.

In the Air and Sea

Pilots fly some robots

by remote control.

The Raven flies over areas

and takes pictures.

Some robots travel underwater.
Bluefin-21 takes pictures
of the ocean floor
and sunken ships.

BALLAST TANK VENT

Glossary

bionic—having to do with mechanical parts made to replace a body part

remote control—a way to control machines from a distance

robot—a machine that can do work and is operated by remote control or a computer

scientist—a person who studies the world around us

sensor—an instrument that notices changes and can send information to a controlling device

sushi—a meal made of vegetables, raw fish, and cold, cooked rice

Read More

Alpert, Barbara. *Military Robots.* Military Machines. North Mankato, Minn.: Capstone Press, 2012.

Hyland, Tony. *Robot World.* Fast Facts. Mankato, Minn.: Sea-to-Sea Publications, 2012.

Internet Sites

FactHound offers a safe, fun way to find Internet sites related to this book. All of the sites on FactHound have been researched by our staff.

Here's all you do:

Visit *www.facthound.com*

Type in this code: 9781491405864

Super-cool stuff! Check out projects, games and lots more at **www.capstonekids.com**

Critical Thinking Using the Common Core

1. Describe ways in which robotic arms may be more useful than real ones. (Integration of Knowledge and Ideas)

2. Why might scientists want to send robots to the ocean floor rather than humans? (Integration of Knowledge and Ideas)

Index

Word Count: 177
Grade: 1
Early-Intervention Level: 17